Green As a Frog
Vert comme une grenouille

written by **Molly Dingles**

illustrated by **Walter Velez**

dingles & company New Jersey

©2004 by Judith Mazzeo Zocchi

All rights reserved.
No part of this book may be reproduced in any form
without written permission from the publishers,
except by a reviewer who may quote brief passages
in a review to be printed in a newspaper or magazine.

First printing

PUBLISHED BY dingles&company

P.O. Box 508 • Sea Girt, New Jersey • 08750
WEBSITE: www.dingles.com • E-MAIL: info@dingles.com

LIBRARY BINDING EDITION DISTRIBUTED BY **GUMDROP BOOKS**
P.O. Box 505 • Bethany, Missouri • 64424
(660) 425-7777

Library of Congress Catalog Card No.: 2004090860
ISBN: 1-891997-71-8

Printed in the United States of America

●

ART DIRECTED & DESIGNED BY Barbie Lambert
ENGLISH EDITED BY Andrea Curley • FRENCH EDITED BY Jonathan Strickland

DEVELOPMENT TEAM
Kathleen P. Miller, Meredith Paril,
Leslie Greenley, Alison Bolte

PREPRESS BY Pixel Graphics, Inc.

For Vincent III

Molly Dingles

is the author of *Jinka Jinka Jelly Bean* and *Little Lee Lee's Birthday Bang*. As Judy Zocchi, she has written the *Paulie & Sasha* series. She is a writer and lyricist who holds a bachelor's degree in fine arts/theater from Mount Saint Mary's College and a master's degree in educational theater from New York University. She lives in Manasquan, New Jersey, with her husband, David.

Walter Velez

was born in New York. He attended the High School of Art and Design and later the School of Visual Arts. He has done illustration work for many major book and gaming companies. He is known for the popular series *Thieves World* as well as the *Myth* series for Ace Books. He has also produced trading cards for *Goosebumps* and *Dune*. In addition, Walter has illustrated several *Star Wars* books for Random House. He lives in Queens, New York, with his wife, Kriti, and daughter, Kassandra.

The Community of Color series is more than just a series of books about colors. The series demonstrates how individual people, places, and things combine to form a community. It allows children to view the world in segments and then experience the wonderment and value of the community as a whole.

Green floppy ferns

●

Vert comme des fougères

Green moss
on the ground

Vert comme
la mousse

Green leaping frog

Vert comme une grenouille qui saute

Green grass
can be found.

Vert comme
le gazon qui pousse.

Green squirming snake

●

Vert comme
un serpent qui se tortille

Green bugs in a bunch

●

Vert comme des bestioles dans un tas

Green gliding moth

Vert comme un papillon qui glisse sur l'air

Green mango for lunch.

Vert comme
une mangue au repas.

Green twisted vines

Vert comme des vignes tordues

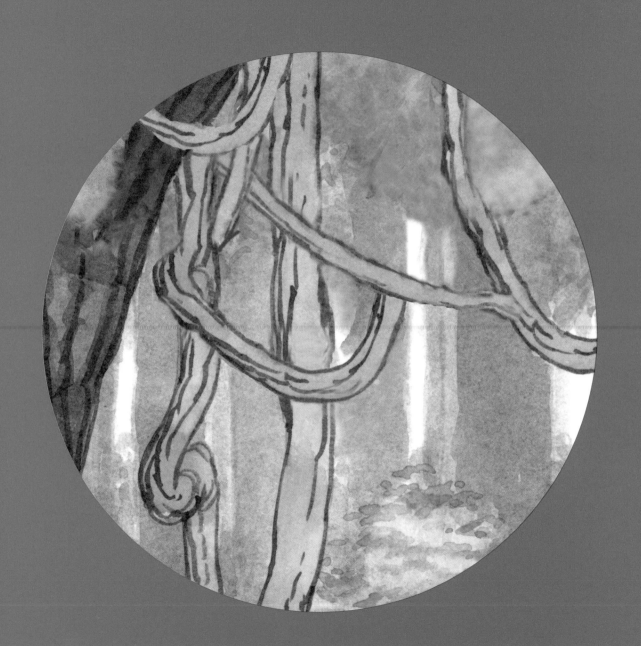

Green parrot in flight

Vert comme
un perroquet qui s'enfuit

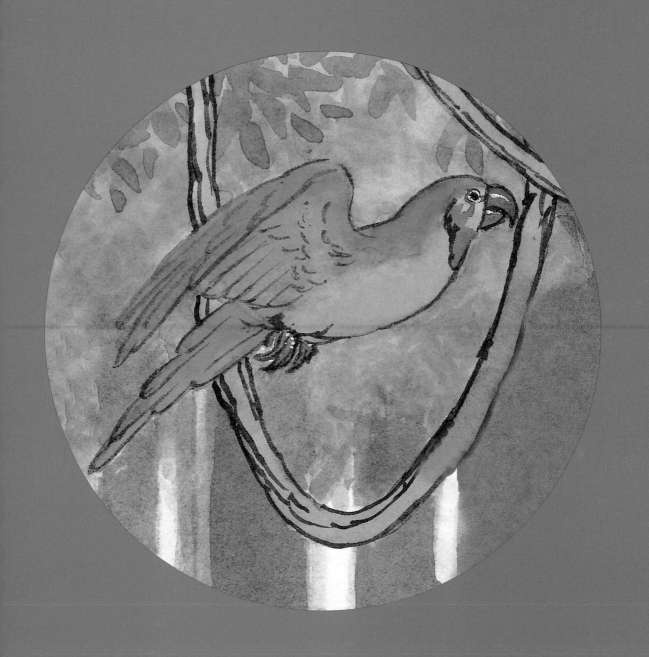

Green X on the map

Vert comme la croix sur la carte

Green tent for the night.

Vert comme la tente
pour la nuit.

The color Green is all around.

On voit
du vert partout.

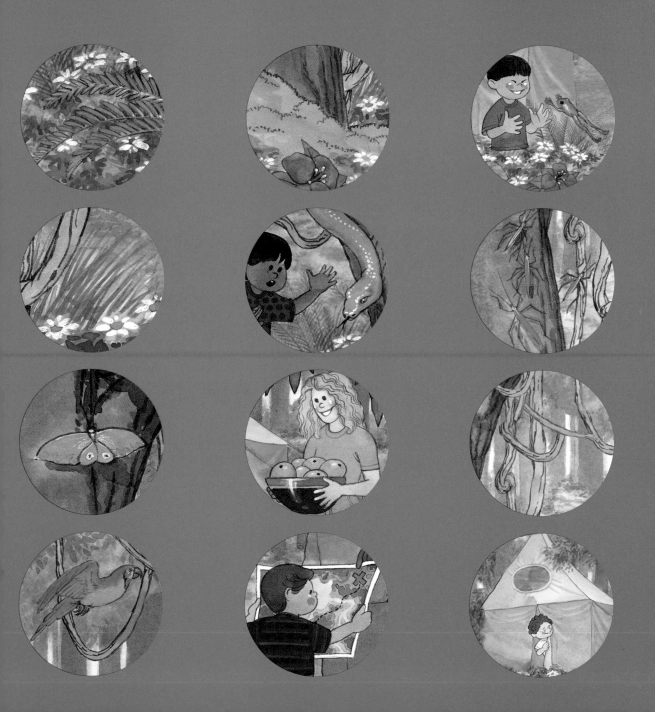

ABOUT COLOR

Use the Community of Color series to teach your child to identify the most basic colors and to help him or her relate these colors to objects in the real world. ASK:

- What color is this book about?
- Can you name all the green things in this jungle scene?
- How many green bugs can you find?
- What green fruit is in this picture?

ABOUT COMMUNITY

Use the Community of Color series to teach your child how he or she is an important part of the community. EXPLAIN TO YOUR CHILD WHAT A COMMUNITY IS:

- A community is a place where people live, work, and play together.
- Your family is a community.
- Your school is a community.
- Your neighborhood is a community.
- The world is one big community.

Everyone plays an important part in making a community work - moms, dads, boys, girls, police officers, firefighters, teachers, mail carriers, garbage collectors, store clerks, and even animals are all important parts of a community. USE THESE QUESTIONS TO FURTHER THE CONVERSATION:

- How are the people in this jungle interacting with one another?
- How are the people different from one another? How are they the same?
- What do they have in common?
- How is the community you see in this book like your community? How is it different?
- Describe your community.

ABOUT FEELINGS

Colors can describe as well as evoke different emotions. Encourage your child to describe the feelings that the color green inspires. ASK:

- How does the color green make you feel?
- Name your favorite green thing in this book. Why is it your favorite?
- Name your favorite green thing at home. Why is it your favorite?
- Can you tell how the people in the picture feel by looking at their faces?
  Do you ever feel the same way? When? Why?

TRY SOMETHING NEW . . . Lend a hand! Plant a tree with green leaves at your school for the community to enjoy (but get permission before you do).